Copyright © 2025 by Charlotte Chang

All rights reserved. No part of this publication may be reproduced, distributed, or transmitted in any form or by any means, including photocopying, recording, or other electronic or mechanical methods, without the prior written permission of the publisher, except in the case of brief quotations embodied in critical reviews and certain other noncommercial uses permitted by copyright law.

ISBN 978-1-998317-95-0

Cover design by Charlotte Chang.

First Edition: December, 2025

Three little pigs had grown up, and it was time for them to live on their own. They waved goodbye to their mom and set off to build their very own homes.

三只小猪长大了，到了要自己生活的时候。他们向猪妈妈挥挥手，出发去盖属于自己的小房子。

**The first little pig found fluffy straw.
"This will be a nice, quick house!" he said, making a soft round hut.**

大猪哥哥找到了一大堆软软的稻草。
"用这个盖房子又快又棒!"
他说着,盖起了一个圆圆的稻草小屋。

The second little pig gathered straight sticks.
"My house will be stronger than straw,"
he said, tapping each stick into place.

二猪弟弟捡来了一大把直直的木棍。
"我的房子一定比稻草更结实!"
他说着,把木棍一根一根固定好。

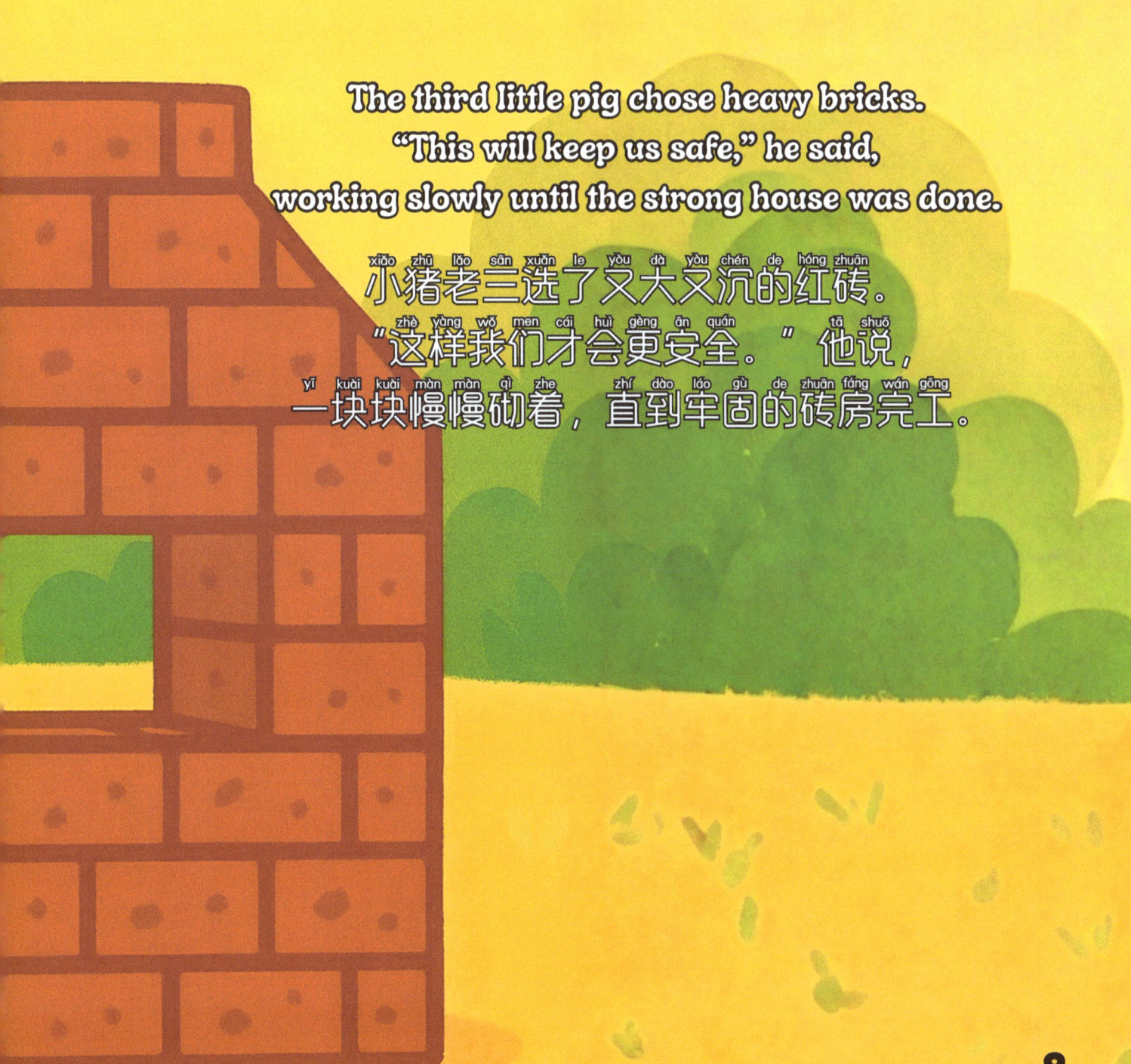

The third little pig chose heavy bricks.
"This will keep us safe," he said,
working slowly until the strong house was done.

小猪老三选了又大又沉的红砖。
"这样我们才会更安全。"他说，
一块块慢慢砌着，直到牢固的砖房完工。

One day, a hungry wolf walked by the straw house.
He sniffed the air.
"Mmm... I smell a little pig," he whispered.

一天，一只饥肠辘辘的大灰狼路过稻草屋。
他动了动鼻子，悄悄嘀咕道：
"嗯……我好像闻到小猪的味道啦。"

The wolf blew a big breath—whooosh!
The straw flew everywhere,
and the first little pig ran away as fast as he could!

大灰狼狠狠吸了一口气——呼!
稻草被吹得到处乱飞,
大猪哥哥赶紧拔腿就跑!

He dashed to the stick house.
"Let me in! The wolf is coming!"
His brother opened the door, and they hid together.

他一路飞奔到木头房子前。
"快开门！大灰狼来了！"
二猪弟弟赶紧把门拉开，两只小猪躲在一起。

The wolf stomped up to the stick house and growled.
He took a big breath... and blew hard!
The door wiggled, but the house didn't fall.

大灰狼气冲冲地走到木头房子前，低声吼了几声。
他深深吸了一大口气……然后用力一吹！
木门摇了摇，但小房子还是稳稳站着。

The wolf stepped back... and BAM!
He crashed his whole body into the stick house.
The sticks rattled and fell apart in a loud clatter!
The two little pigs ran for their lives.

大灰狼往后退了几步……
然后"砰"地一下撞向木头房子!
木棍被撞得一阵乱响,哗啦啦全散开了。
两只小猪吓得转身就跑。

The two little pigs hurried to the brick house.
Their brother welcomed them in and locked the sturdy door tight.

两只小猪连忙向砖房跑去。
小猪老三赶紧把他们请进来,并把结实的门关得紧紧的。

The wolf stood in front of the brick house and puffed as hard as he could. Nothing moved.

大灰狼站在砖房前,用尽全力吹啊吹。
可房子纹丝不动。

So he tried the other way.
He leaned back and thumped his shoulder into the door.
"Ow!" he yelped.
The brick house didn't even shake.

于是,他换了个办法。
大灰狼往后一仰,用肩膀猛地撞向大门。
"哎哟!"他痛得叫了一声。
可砖房一点都没晃。

The wolf was getting grumpy.
He crawled onto the roof, slow and sneaky.
He stretched his neck and peeked toward the chimney.

大灰狼有点不高兴了。
他慢慢、悄悄地爬上了屋顶。
伸长脖子,往烟囱里面偷看。

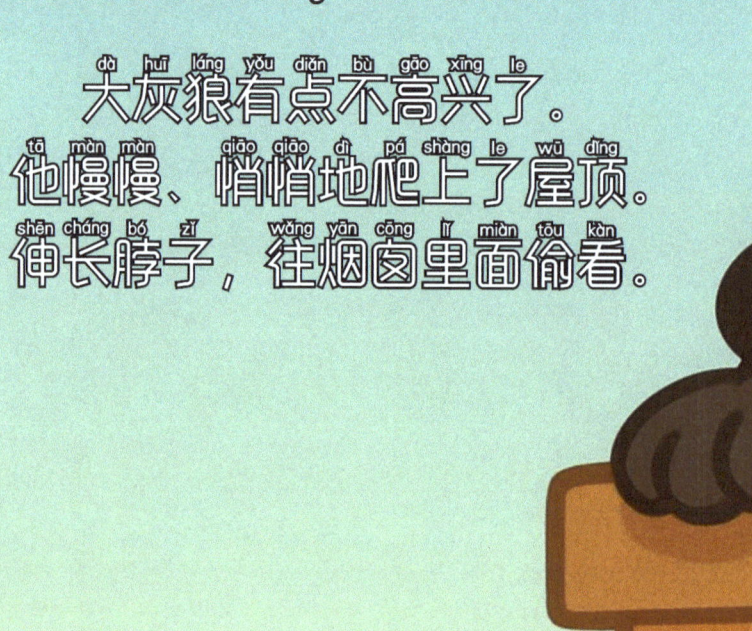

Inside, the little pigs spotted him.
"Quick! Light the fire!" whispered the third pig.
A warm flame crackled,
and puffs of smoke drifted upward toward the wolf.

屋子里的小猪们一下就发现了他。
"快点！生火！"小猪老三轻声说。
火苗"啪啦啪啦"地跳起来，
一缕缕烟慢慢往上飘，直冲大灰狼。

The wolf yelped, scrambled off the roof, and ran far, far away.
The three little pigs hugged tight.
"We're safe now," said the third pig.

And from that day on, they lived happily together in the cozy brick house.

大灰狼被烟呛得直叫，连忙从屋顶爬下来，落荒而逃。
三只小猪紧紧抱在一起。
小猪老三说："现在安全了。"

从那天起，他们就在温暖的砖房里，一起开始了开心的生活。

www.ingramcontent.com/pod-product-compliance
Lightning Source LLC
LaVergne TN
LVHW070453080526
838202LV00035B/2820